The Sources of Inspiration of Anthroposophy

The Sources of Inspiration of Anthroposophy

Sigismund von Gleich

TEMPLE LODGE
London

Translated by Hans Christof Valentien and Muriel Valentien
Translation edited by J. Collis

17/98

Temple Lodge Publishing
51 Queen Caroline Street
London W6 9QL

Published by Temple Lodge 1997

Originally published in German under the title *Die Inspirations-Quellen der Anthroposophie* by Mellinger Verlag, Stuttgart, in 1981

A catalogue record for this book is available from the British Library

ISBN 0 904693 87 2

Cover by S. Gulbekian
Typeset by DP Photosetting, Aylesbury, Bucks
Printed and bound in Great Britain by Cromwell Press Limited, Broughton Gifford, Wiltshire

Contents

Foreword

Although *The Sources of Inspiration of Anthroposophy* was written in the early 1950s, its message seems to me more relevant than ever now that the century is drawing to a close. I have felt for some time that this rich, deep 'document' should be available also for English readers, and I am grateful that this has become possible in the centenary year of the author's birth. In Sigismund von Gleich's own words, 'this sketch is not meant as a theoretical representation of certain truths but to help those who feel it could become fruitful to work with these truths, to become inwardly connected to them.' This was his last written work, completed at Easter, 1953, six months before his death.

Hans Christof Valentien
Christmas 1996

Towards the Deepening of Spiritual Endeavour

Whatever has been founded on earth out of spiritual sources can only remain alive and fruitful for our fellow human beings if again and again it can draw nourishment from those original sources. Without such enlivening, what has been founded is in danger of being diluted into the non-essential and then disappearing, or of becoming fixed in a form conditioned by a particular period. As dogma it then hinders the further development demanded by altered conditions of other times. There are plenty of examples of this in earlier or even more recent history. Many important spiritual creations have either faded into mere 'literature' or hardened into mere doctrines. Only something which in the flowing stream of time can change itself out of its own inner life, finding in each moment the connection to its original source — only such a thing can remain always in accord with the times and be ensouled by ever-youthful life.

Rudolf Steiner, the founder of anthroposophy, always strove for a living enhancement of what had been already brought forward. Because of this, what he was able to give mankind in the course of forty years, corresponding to the inner and outer circumstances of the world, appeared again and again in different forms although in essence it remained the same from beginning to end: the new revelation of the being of man in its connection with the divine beings of the world.

Not infrequently that step-by-step unfolding of anthroposophy and its impulses for practical life led to very surprising changes of direction, just as the history of mankind itself changes in leaps. Some found it difficult at times to follow the spiritual leader with understanding and willing cooperation when once again his way of working had changed or taken a new turn.

What a leap in history was the beginning of the decisive period of world catastrophes — not at all recognized as such at the time: the outbreak of the First World War! More important, however, are the hidden turning-points of inner history which can only be recognized through spiritual insight.

The spiritual situation of mankind became profoundly changed at the dawning of the Age of Light (1900) after five thousand years in which the human soul had been closed off from experiencing the spiritual world; but also at the beginning of the new inspiration out of the Sun-spirit realm about twenty years earlier. It is after all thanks to those Spirit-events that Rudolf Steiner was able from 1880 onwards to prepare anthroposophy methodically and then, from the beginning of our century onwards, to speak about it!

Yet only a short time later the signs of the times were again different. Around 1909 those new impulses became effective to whose apocalyptic meaning for present and future times he pointed from then onwards. Thirty years after the beginning of the new Age of Michael, the new Appearance of Christ shone out within the etheric realm of the earth. For that new Christ Age the archangel of the sun, mighty in spirit, had prepared the way from heaven to earth. In face of these imminent spiritual events, Rudolf Steiner had given profound revelations about the wisdom of the Gospels from 1908 onwards. He defined the characteristics of the approaching new revelation of Christ. The deeply moving revelations about the 'fifth Gospel' were one special fruit of this.[1]

Already then (1909) his listeners were being prepared for that greatest of all events which, fifty years after Michael's victory, as its mature fruit, was to start putting forth shoots in order to become fully effective in the second half of the century. Christ was to become, so it was proclaimed, the Inspirer of conscience and Lord and Master of the web of human destiny which out of His grace could be altered and ordered anew.

Now this time has already dawned. Christ is already acting as the Lord of Karma![2]

But meanwhile, probably earlier and more forcefully than was originally foreseen, the counter-forces, too, have stepped on to the scene, especially since the important year 1933 in which also the catastrophe of the Second World War began to prepare itself. What since then has become an unending unfolding of power in Central Europe has distracted mankind's thought and conscience in the most fateful way from the imminent, new effects of Christ's grace.

Graver still is the fact that Rudolf Steiner was not able to experience on earth that decisive moment of spiritual history. That he left the physical plane 25 years before the second half of the century—therein lies an unspeakable tragedy. Even a temporary victory of the counter-forces on the physical plane after 1933 would possibly not have had such terribly destructive effects if anthroposophists had been carrying out their obligations properly from 1923 onwards, of which they had often been reminded.

Looking at those important years, an earnest examination of our conscience could well cause each one of us to apply to him or herself the call of the Baptist which is renewed today in the new Christ Age. *Metanoeite! Repent! Change your hearts!*

*

Rudolf Steiner would have reached the patriarchal age in 1933. How might he have spoken since? How would he have spoken in the thirties, in the forties or from the beginning of the second half of our century! Probably no one can imagine the immeasurable greatness and spirit-earnestness of this.

This is by no means a superfluous question today, as we approach the decisive end of the century. It can, in fact, awaken definite resolves in one's heart. There is one thing on which we can surely all agree: We want with all our strength and devotion to reflect quite anew on the spiritual sources of anthroposophy in order to enable ourselves faithfully to further spiritual knowledge as something vitally alive. Connecting ourselves in meditation with these sources we will perhaps become able, in face of the enormous decisions of the present hour, to find the right ways of carrying out spiritual scientific activity until the end of the century.

Did not Rudolf Steiner once say in connection with Christianity, 'From time to time other revelations will come for which we must keep our minds open ...'?[3]

*

Since Rudolf Steiner worked out of the original sources in ever changing ways, in keeping with the spiritual demands of the times, we may be convinced that from 1950 onwards it will be decisive whether or not all spiritual scientific life and endeavour tries to do justice to those new deeds of Christ within the supersensible realm which have been proclaimed to us. What a spur to moral self-awareness! What an obligation to change one's attitude could arise from this awareness! But also what enthusiasm can be kindled in open hearts when they begin to divine in which new spirit anthroposophy should be lived today and in the future!

In face of the assistance newly streaming down to us from Christ which the spiritual leader has revealed, is not anthroposophy becoming more than ever a sublime service to God in the consciousness that we can serve, honestly and reverently, this working of Christ? Therefore today those words speak to our hearts, more earnestly binding than ever, in which Rudolf Steiner—leaving aside his usual moderation—once found it necessary to tell the friends what anthroposophy actually is. We take this quotation from the 1916 cycle of lectures *Toward Imagination*:

'Very often, my dear friends, I am asked by our members: How do I connect myself with Christ? This is a naïve question! For all we can strive for, every line which we read of our anthroposophical science, connects us with Christ. *We do, as it were, nothing else!*'[4]

However, consider the *what*, but consider more the *how*. We need to tend the spiritual-scientific truths radiating towards us from the words with the same reverence with which we would perhaps stand in spirit before the Redeemer of mankind should we be honoured by His Presence. Only then will we do justice in our mood of soul to the being of anthroposophy in the time when the Christ Spirit is working anew, full of blessing, out of the spiritual world. Probably in looking at the imminence of this nearness of Christ, Rudolf Steiner stressed towards the end of his activity on earth: 'Thus anthroposophy begins everywhere with science, enlivens its perceptions through art and *ends with religious deepening*; begins with what the head can grasp, approaches what in the widest sense can form the word, and ends with what permeates the heart with warmth, leading it to certainty, in order that the soul of man at all times may find itself in its true home in the realm of spirit. Thus, my dear friends, we should learn on the path of anthroposophy to start from knowledge, lift ourselves up to art and end in religious inwardness.'[5] Without doubt this holds good for the anthroposophical path of the individual as well as for the development of the anthroposophical movement as a whole.

Similar words were spoken at that time to the generation of youth which would become fully mature around the middle of the century. 'We must come so far that all life achieves this religious quality, is permeated by this religious quality.'[6] In the same connection another appeal, now more timely than ever, was addressed to everyone, young and old, awakening true self-knowledge: 'In the innermost depths, in the innermost part of the soul we must search for light, above all seek to come to the deepest, innermost feeling for honesty and truth. If we build on honesty and truthfulness, then we shall make progress.'

All anthroposophical work should proceed out of the consciousness soul. However, perhaps too little known or taken to heart is an indication of Rudolf Steiner's characterizing the forces forming the consciousness soul, enabling it to receive the spirit-self, which is indeed decisive today: 'Love is one part of devotion and submission is the other part. Thus submission becomes the teacher of the consciousness soul. Devotion is to stream forth from the ego towards what is to be recognized. Only that feeling of reverence which is glowed through by the ego, the submission in which we immerse ourselves, taking the ego with us—only that can be healing for the human soul.'[7]

The Fivefold Stream of Inspiration out of the Spiritual World

Only under certain conditions, it seems to me, will one manage during the second half of the century to cultivate anthroposophy in a worthy way, maintaining its vital creativity. Above all, students of Rudolf Steiner should be fully aware of their obligation to experience the wisdom of spiritual knowledge at all times as proceeding from their teacher, and to represent it in this way. With this no mere formality is meant but the consciousness, ever again renewed, that in representing this spiritual endowment we remain personally responsible to Rudolf Steiner.

Those who want to work *out* of anthroposophy and not merely report on it should always remember the man who once embodied it but who also continues to carry and inspire it as a living being. Can one really represent it worthily without this spiritual support? Although the content of anthroposophy expresses nothing else but full reality, including its spiritual side, its living stream of inspiration out of the spiritual world nonetheless continues to be further mediated through the inaugurator. To keep anthroposophy alive and creatively develop it further will be possible all the sooner, the more inwardly a relationship of gratitude and remembrance with its founder is cultivated.

Therefore it could well become an ideal for some of us to keep the creator-genius of spiritual science in mind throughout our daily activities. Of course these daily duties demand one's full attention. A comparison can show what is meant. As a deeply impressive melody sometimes does not leave us but quietly and effectively resounds in our soul's depths all day long, so might such a resolve be shaped. Perhaps at the transition from one activity to another this remembering would rise out of the quiet background into full consciousness for moments during the day.

Those who feel the need to be continuously connected with the teacher and inspirer of spiritual wisdom, and responsible to him, would soon experience good and fruitful impulses arising from within. In contrast, those who wanted to reproduce this spiritual substance without thinking of its inspirer would start to separate work and impulse from its creator. The de-humanizing of thought-contents is one of the main goals of that adversary who wants to rob the human being of his ego. Yet since the uniting of Christ with the earth and mankind, all the spirituality of the world is meant to be reborn out of the human ego in order that the cosmos will be humanized through and through!

*

Even though anthroposophy has appeared as the free creative deed of a unique, great human spirit, ultimately it arises nonetheless out of specific exceedingly high sources of inspiration from the divine spiritual world to which Rudolf Steiner has paved the way. He himself owes it to those high spiritual powers that the content of anthroposophy could be spoken about.

Already in the book *Theosophy* he emphasized: 'The work of the spiritual scientist in his own soul, which gives him the faculty of clairvoyance, goes towards attaining this faculty. Whether or not he then perceives something in the spiritual world in a particular case—that does not any more depend on him; it flows to him as a gift out of the spiritual world. He cannot force it, he must wait until it comes about.'

This holds good in small things as in big, and in the highest degree for the deepest truths which Rudolf Steiner could impart. He owed them to the higher powers. In this connection the following indication is important: 'In the present time it is necessary to suppress the craving to know. Rather one should say to oneself: Grace has brought me a number of truths and I will patiently wait until further truths come to me. Today a certain passive attitude towards truth is really more necessary than perhaps even twenty years ago ... This is practical instruction as regards the investigation of the spiritual worlds, especially in relation to the Christ Event.'[8] Without doubt one may and should enquire about the spiritual sources of inspiration of anthroposophy.

To guard anthroposophy from too much intellectuality, and keep it alive in its further development, we must not only strive for an intimate connection with its founder but also cultivate a deep reverence, a meditative contact with the impulses and beings of the divine spiritual world working as inspiring and effective powers behind its earthly expression. Because Rudolf Steiner found access to these powers and was blessed by them, he was able to give these impulses expression in his work. Therefore we can also find them in his work.

One's search for truth and work through anthroposophy are enlivened and made inward when, next to study and meditative self-education, one takes the trouble to establish such contacts. Through this the connection to the living powers of origin of spiritual science will certainly be found ever anew. In the dawn of the new Christ Age those spiritual sources will stream down to mankind on earth in an ever richer and stronger way. For the Christ Spirit remains forever connected with mankind in infinite love, being closest with His help when mankind has to stand up to the most difficult trials of the soul.

*

Which impulses in the work of Rudolf Steiner now arise so clearly as the decisive ones that we can fittingly call them the divine, living arteries of his work? It is not enough only to point to the Christ Impulse. For on closer consideration it becomes apparent that four other Spirit Impulses work together with it, all of which have their centre, their heart, in the Christ Impulse itself.

Essentially there are five fundamental impulses that come to expression in anthroposophy. In their organic unity and manifold cooperation they form the totality of the new Christ Impulse. Without much difficulty one can recognize yet further impulses merely as the effects of these five main ones; for example, the impulse of freedom or of art.

Most intimately connected with the central, actual Christ Impulse is, first of all, the new Michael Impulse. Intimately connected with both is the Grail Impulse. But behind this, as we will show, stands the Sophia Impulse. Through Christ, the Sophia will be reborn in the human being, and this Sophia lets Christ appear to man in a new light. Of especially great importance at the very time when Christ is becoming Lord and Transformer of Karma, as so often mentioned by Rudolf Steiner, will be the Impulse of the Beings of Karma. Already in the last year of his life this inspiration out of the sphere of the karmic beings came to especially powerful expression in profound revelations about the truths of reincarnation and karma.

All these impulses proceed, as it is easy to see, from quite specific beings, from very high and sublime divine powers.

To such lofty beings, to archangels such as Michael and Uriel, and to the still much higher beings of the divine Sophia, of Christ and the Powers of Karma in the highest hierarchy, one can raise oneself meditatively in the right sense only when one's heart is wholly filled with feelings of worship and devotion.

*

The present time is exceedingly grave; the future will bring the most severe trials of destiny and hardship. Who would deny that we have already failed much too often with regard to our immense spiritual duties? Who would not need assistance from above for his or her own spiritual endeavours?

The instruction of Christ remains true and will become ever more true, no less for those striving for spiritual science: Ask, and it shall be given to you; seek, and you shall find; knock, and it shall be opened unto you.

Intellect alone can never fruitfully receive the sacred life-breath of Spirit wisdom. Everyone needs the eye of the heart, the feeling for truth, the intuitively spiritualized power of thought and moral fantasy or the germinating power of Imagination as organs of perception. These forces can stream towards each one of us out of the living sources of inspiration from which all wisdom arises. Ultimately, wisdom can only be grasped and represented out of the strength of its original sources. For like can only be recognized by like.

Only someone in whose heart something is already stirring of the new Christ-Michael Impulse can sense this life-blood within anthroposophy. Only someone who in the undefiled part of his soul is gripped by a deep longing for the soul's sacred, starry origin — only such a person will feel in himself the urge for higher knowledge and will also have an organ that can sense the form of the Sophia revelation suitable to our time.

Only a heart able to permeate itself through and through with that spiritual power which dwells within the inspiring, original impulses of spiritual science can truly live in accordance with the spirit in thoughts, words and deeds.

Let us therefore attempt to present in their organic totality the Spirit Impulses which are clearly to be recognized in the work of Rudolf Steiner. It can only be a sketch whose contents may well be supplemented from various points of view.

However, this sketch is not meant as a theoretical

representation of certain truths but to help those who also feel it could become fruitful to work with these truths, to become inwardly connected with them. Precisely in this way the pupil's work comes into harmony with that of his teacher, even when the two are living physically separated from each other.

I
The Christ Impulse

We recognize and revere in the Christ Spirit the Word that in the beginning was with God and Itself was God. Through It has everything been created. Step by step in the creation of the world the Word became life and light of soul for man and all creatures.

At the festival of Whitsun His holy ego-fire sacrificed Itself into mankind. The Christ Spirit is the original source of human existence in the image of God. He is both the cosmic origin of the being of man, and the light of the world. When out of the wounds of the Crucified One His blood streamed down to earth, there flowed into mankind with this blood Christ's infinite Being of Love, so that in human beings the power of true freedom may germinate.

Infinite and incomprehensibly deep is the secret of the Son and His sacrifice for mankind. Immeasurably great and far-reaching is His effectiveness for the coming evolution of the world and mankind. A free act of grace was the becoming of the Son, a free act of grace was His sacrifice. Therefore the acceptance of Christ as the Son of God connected to mankind is possible only through a free act of the human soul.

'To the Father God Christ comes as a free creation. As a creation which does not follow Him immediately but which puts itself next to the preceding creation as a free deed which also had the possibility not to exist ... The Son has been given to the world as a free deed, through grace, through freedom, through love which gives itself freely in its creation. Thus philosophical-logical necessity leads us indeed to the recognition of the Father but not of Christ ... To recognize Christ in Him Who was there as

Christ, we have to exert an energetic impulse for truth; that has to be our free deed. This very thing is the higher truth, which does not force us, which is our free deed: the truth in which we believe brought to its highest point.'[9] 'The event of Golgotha is a free, cosmic deed arising out of World-love; it can be comprehended only by human love.'[10]

In addition, Rudolf Steiner quoted Soloviev's religious views: 'No philosophy, no natural science can connect the realm of grace with existence; for the forces of nature work mechanically and the forces of thought have only the reality of thought. So what does possess that full reality which can connect the soul with immortality? The personal Christ working in the world has this full reality; and only the living Christ—not the one merely experienced in thought—can give the answer. The one merely effective in the soul (in thought) would, after all, leave the soul alone; for the soul cannot on its own give birth to the realm of grace.' Thus we are obliged—of this Soloviev would be convinced—to believe in Christ, for otherwise we negate ourselves and call our existence a lie. But one can only achieve this through one's own free deed![11]

In his essay on 'the image of Christ as a test of conscience' Soloviev gave some advice that should be taken very seriously: 'The best and only test is after all so near at hand! Before we decide on any action that is of importance in personal or public life, we only need to call up in our soul the image of Christ, to concentrate on this image and ask ourselves, "Could He do this act?"—or, in other words—"Does He find it good or not? Does He give me His blessing in this deed or not?" I advise everyone to make this test—and no one will be deceived ... Remind yourself of Christ, imagine Him alive before you as He actually is. If everyone ... were to start from now on, filled with good will, to turn to this unfailing guidance in all cases of doubt, then this would be the beginning of His Coming again and the preparation for the Last Judgment of Christ — for the time is now very close.'[12]

The human being of today has to guard especially against two main errors: either to see God only in his own human entity or not to want to recognize Him at all. The first leads to arrogance, the second to despair. Pascal already had to warn about this. However, Christ has pointed the way to find God — Christ Who has been like man, Who has lived with human beings.

In coming times of hardship, arrogance and despair will rob many people of the blessings of the new Christ Impulse. Therefore the soul should deeply imbue itself with Rudolf Steiner's way of pointing to Christ for the second half of the century: 'The only healing of pride is when one directs one's gaze to the God Who submitted to the Cross; when the soul looks to Christ submitting Himself to death on the Cross. But this is also the only way of healing all despair. For humility is not something that makes one weak; it gives a healing power reaching beyond all despair. As mediator between pride and despair the Helper, the Saviour, in the sense of Pascal, arises in the human soul. Every human being can feel this even without clairvoyance. This is the preparation for Christ Who will be visible for all human beings from the twentieth century on, resurrecting in every human breast as the Healer of pride and despair, Who could not be felt in the same way earlier.'[13]

*

Again and again in the course of time the counter-forces have made the greatest efforts to stifle the new divine spark which the Saviour on Golgotha kindled in human souls. Since the end of the last century they have become overpowering. In future they will do their utmost to distract human beings from Christ through arrogance and despair. Christ remained true to mankind even when it scoffed at Him through a materialistic denial of the spirit. But in this way He has taken upon Himself the 'death of the soul' which is a consequence of the denial of the spirit. He Himself experienced it in the supersensible realm like a repeated crucifixion, like an isolation in the darkening of consciousness — for there is no death in the spiritual world.

But the higher, eternal life of the Resurrected One remains forever the victor over all powers of death and darkness. 'For the dying of the Christ Consciousness within the sphere of angels in the nineteenth century means the resurrection of the direct Christ Consciousness in human beings. That is: From the twentieth century on, the life of Christ will be felt more and more as a personal experience in human souls.'[14]

Christ emerged with heightened forces of life and enlightenment from the second 'crucifixion' in the super-sensible world; and today He is already quickening human beings with new waters of life and promising new blessings for the near future. This certainty might be formulated briefly thus:

'Know, O man, the new Spirit of Christ in the living and immeasurable stream of His new promise and love!'

But shall we learn to drink from that divine fountain?

Undoubtedly not, if we were to remain unable to create that special moral atmosphere which, as Rudolf Steiner repeatedly pointed out, is the pre-condition for recognizing the effectiveness of the new Christ Impulse among human beings. How should the eternal Gospel of Love, which will emanate from the Spirit Presence of Christ, realize itself on earth if people do not want to cooperate in suitable ways?

If among human beings the will to understand and for-give, the readiness for reconciliation, the will to carry mutually each other's burdens of destiny and to take on new spiritual duties — if all this were to flare up like a holy flame then, in this flame of offering, the new working of Christ as Lord and Transformer of Karma would soon become effective in a healing way. We cannot go on any longer without the active moral cooperation of people on earth who are of good will, however blind they may have remained in other ways.

We shall here refrain from going into the question of how Christ affects the destinies of those not incarnated at present. But also among the souls now incarnated, the grace of karmic help leading beyond deadlocks in destiny will sooner or later want to become effective. In this, voluntary decisions out of moral intuitions must surely play their part.

On account of strongly contrary headwinds and hurricanes, the steering of a person's boat of life can today become uncertain; in consequence the boat of life can become so firmly stranded on a sandbank that one can hardly set it afloat again out of one's own strength. In such cases from now on—so we may suppose—the 'miracle' might come about that the divine Lord of Karma, for the sake of a higher necessity, loosens the little boat from the sandbank. With a simultaneous change of soul such a person is thus given the possibility of new freedom of movement.

But if a readiness for reconciliation based on deep understanding is not developed among human beings, then the associates of such an unfortunate one might be those who do not understand the change of heart and the new course of life embarked on. Not trusting, they can then only hinder his transformation. Hardly anything works so disastrously among human beings as the fatal tendency to nail someone down to earlier ways of action or traits of character which have perhaps recently, or even long since, been overcome. This lovelessness, a rigidity out of self-complacency or love of ease, this it is whereby people continuously nail down—and crucify—one another.

If we could only henceforth believe unshakeably in the ability for change in our fellow human beings! Without such a faith in Damascus miracles in the moral sphere—a faith that can move mountains—brought about through the grace of the etheric Christ, we shall not advance one single step. Never shall we understand the new Christ era in its uniqueness as something that has never been before, if within ourselves the power of trust in our fellow human beings does not grow far beyond the common measure.

How else can it become possible for thoroughly opposite kinds of human beings or streams of mankind (such as that of Cain and Abel), which we meet everywhere, to be reconciled in order to work with instead of against each other? Perhaps Albert Steffen meant precisely this when he wrote about the pre-condition for a reconciliation between Cain and Abel, between Hiram and Solomon: 'If the one lives in the other, and each one wakes up through the other, then they will work together and realize the heavenly Jerusalem on earth as planned by Melchizedek, the King of Justice.'[15]

A disposition of wanting to build bridges between opposites could become extremely fruitful also on a large scale in all fields of life in community. How else but in purely human ways will the abysmal, hate-filled mistrust between the peoples of East and West be overcome?

In the long run all problems of social life could be solved, and thereby ideological tensions removed, if the ideas of threefoldness could be tackled out of this disposition. It would lead to the establishment of quite new forms of community and groupings within mankind, forms whose life-blood would be esteem for the brother with whom one works, appreciation of his human dignity, large-hearted, full understanding of his special life situation. Groupings such as national states, party organizations, and so on, often long since grown rigid and degenerated into untrue outer forms, work more to separate people than to bring them together. They ought to disappear soon to make room for new forms of community, so that an expression of the original human impulses can first of all become possible again.

Knots of destiny that have tied themselves up so disastrously since the eighteenth century should be undone again today. This will become possible to the degree that responsible leading people let their moral intuitions arise out of trust in the Lord of Life Who wants to dissolve all such disastrous knots with the cooperation of men and women of goodwill.

*

Henceforth Christ works through the human being, in the human being and for the human being. Those who do not believe in the *human being* within each one of us do not, today, truly believe in Christ!

II
The Impulse of the Powers of Karma

By far the most encouraging of all Christian perspectives of the future which Rudolf Steiner has opened up is this: *Christ will henceforth work as the Lord of Karma.*

How should the disastrous entanglements of destiny in world history, that since the last century have led from catastrophe to catastrophe, be untangled before it is too late without the help of higher powers offering mankind, almost hopelessly lost, a new chance to work in a free and good way? Ever more burning becomes the question as to how the highest Genius of freedom and grace, the divine Friend of man, may influence the course of destiny in large and small matters for human beings, for those living on the earth as well as those in the supersensible realm.

Right from the beginning the knowledge of reincarnation and karma formed the nucleus of the spiritual science of man. Of course it did, for the unfolding or self-realization of the human being takes place through reincarnation and karma in the course of epochs, in harmony with God's high plan of education which He carries out through great world-historical Spirit Impulses.

In 1912, long before characterizing this knowledge as the basic essence of spiritual science in the classic karma lectures of 1924, Rudolf Steiner had already stated this to be the core of his mission: '*Most fundamental is the form which the Christ question is given through the fact that reincarnation and karma are taken up in the hearts of human beings. The light which falls upon the Christ question under the assumption of the truths of reincarnation and karma, that is the essential thing.*'[16]

The importance of these words can hardly be over-estimated! Immeasurably high beings of the Father-hierarchy regulate all human destinies according to world justice, both as fruits of one's own deeds and suffering, and also regarding the requirements of world evolution flowing from the 'eternal intentions and goals' of the Godhead. It is almost impossible for the sense-bound intellect to form an idea of the exaltedness and majesty of Cherubim and Seraphim. Profoundly moved by the overwhelming glory of the starry heavens we begin to divine something of the creative might of the powers of karma. In life between death and a new birth we see this in a reversed way. Rudolf Steiner described as follows the spiritual view of the activity of the first hierarchy in creating karma: 'We look upon these Seraphim, Cherubim and Thrones as here we look up to the clouds, the blue sky, the starry heavens. Below us we see Heaven, created out of the activity of Seraphim, Cherubim and Thrones. What kind of activity? While we are between death and a new birth we see in the Seraphim, Cherubim and Thrones that which shows itself as the right harmonizing activity resulting from our own earthly deeds and experiences of life and those we had together with others.'[17]

Two factors determine the formation of destiny and the course of reincarnation for each human being: the personal, and the general historical determining of destiny which is above the personal. The one makes possible the clearing away of old life-debts with regard to one's fellow human beings through atonement or suffering, and gives the chance for a change for the better. The other, however, places the individual in a meaningful way into mankind at large. For here the high karma beings work in harmony with the divine Sophia's *plan of world evolution,* having created each human being as a special divine thought with a specific number of spiritual tasks in the sense of the 'eternal intentions and aims' of the Godhead. Therefore each one of us has to make his own contribution towards realizing all great ideals of mankind by which it grows towards its overall goal. Through this, human spirits are connected in a much deeper sense, for we are karmically indebted to each other not only in a personal way. From the aspect of spiritual world history, due to the similarity or equality of our overall life-tasks, we are members of higher karmic life-communities which have to be recognized and put in order.

Our obligations arising from the working of karma beyond the personal and in the world-historical course of incarnation are decisive today when out of the domain of life Christ wants to unify all human beings, also those belonging to opposite streams.[18]

*

Already in the first lecture cycle At the Gates of Spiritual Science[19] (1906) Rudolf Steiner pointed to the fact that the reality of Christ and the truth of karma belong together. He also pointed to the karma-solidarity which is to be striven for. Let us recall some sentences referring to this: 'The deed of Christ Jesus upon earth will become effective through building on karma. The Redeemer knows that through karma the work of redemption will become accessible to all. Yes, this deed occurred precisely in building upon the Karma Law as a cause for the glorious effect in future, as a seed for a later harvest, as a help for those who let the blessings of redemption work upon themselves ... The testament of Christ Jesus is the teaching of reincarnation and karma. For it is not said: Each must bear the consequences of his deeds, but: The consequences of deeds must be borne, no matter by whom. As here in physical life a brother or friend can step in for someone, so in a much deeper sense can this take place in the spiritual world!'

This indication becomes of greatest consequence today when Christ has become Lord and healing, transforming Master of the web of destiny. Perhaps one may assume that in future, out of the new power of Christ, changes of direction can be brought about for human beings on tragic paths of destiny even while they are on earth, if others can be found who are selflessly ready to help in situations of karmic hindrance.

Our thoughts are led in this direction by certain indications as to the future which Rudolf Steiner gave in the eleventh lecture of *The Gospel of St Matthew*. Here he spoke about the question of 'binding and loosing' with regard to the forgiveness of sin out of Christ's power. Strikingly, a connecting line is drawn from the first apostolic founding of the Christian community of human beings (building on the Spirit Individuality of St Peter) right up to the present time. Here, through Steiner's knowledge of karma, this question might be grasped much more deeply and presumably also dealt with. We can quote only the fundamental sentences:

'Once people understand what Christ is in the same sense in which the better nature of St Peter understands it, then they will set up not only such communities, such orderings as rest upon the kinship of consanguinity, but also those consciously weaving the bond of love from soul to soul. This means that as in the Jewish blood, in the threads that passed through the generations, was woven together what was to be joined within the human race as a whole after the model of the macrocosm ... so now in ethical-moral-spiritual relationships there should come about out of the conscious ego that which separates human beings or holds them together in love. The orderings among human beings should be formed or harmonized out of the conscious ego. When we consider this, we must say: The communities human beings found must be meaningful for them. Speaking anthroposophically we can say: *Individual karma must connect itself with the karma of communities.* In the same way that it does not contradict the idea of karma if I give something to a poor person, just as little does it contradict the idea of karma if an individual's karma is lifted from him by a community. *The community can share the lot of the individual.* Thus a net is woven by the karmic threads of single individuals into the karma of a whole society! And through what Christ has brought down out of spiritual heights this net shall be an image of the order in Heaven. This means: In accordance with the ordering of the spiritual world the karma of the individual shall be connected with the karma of the whole, not in an arbitrary way but so that the community organism will become an image of the order in Heaven ... It is, so to speak, the foundation of mankind of the future built on the nature of the ego.'[20]

*

These words were spoken two septennates before the year 1924. They express the ideal of a human community whose members are willing to carry each other's karmic difficulties in a brotherly way! Rudolf Steiner spoke of different kinds of community, even of 'society'! What with regard to St Peter was still a promise can now be fully realized in the service of and out of the power of the Lord of Karma through the new knowledge of karma and Christ in the present time, if only we strive in this direction. For instance, communities who take as an example to be followed the attitude of someone like Gandhi, who always felt responsible for the mistakes of his fellow human beings and friends—such communities could gradually become 'organs' to be used by Christ, the all-compassionate Transformer and Healer of disordered and tragic connections of destiny. Entirely new kinds of spiritual duties, perceived out of moral intuition and adopted voluntarily, could also be taken on by someone full of enthusiasm and with gratitude for Christ's never-ending deeds of sacrifice.

But the above sentences seem to indicate something else as well. The people of Israel of olden times formed a community of 'warriors of God' (that is the meaning of the word 'Israel') founded on consanguinity through the cosmic laws of nature. Now, in a karmic reversal of this, a community of free individuals shall develop in the spirit of Christ, prepared in their souls to step in for each other so that the ordering and harmonizing of karmic relationships can come about. This, too, was mentioned in the year 1924.

It will certainly be fruitful if many people ponder these connections which are here merely indicated. Only then will justice be done to the way Rudolf Steiner serves the truth of karma in the spirit of Christ's deed of redemption. Only then will the truth of karma become the testament of Christ for the future.

This could be of great help in first of all bringing about the right atmosphere of moral ether forces in which the Spirit of Christ can heal patterns of destiny in quite a new way. The important thing today is the awakening of a readiness to help our fellow human beings to a degree that has never been there before, going far beyond the normal measure of morality. Those who have wakened up to the Spirit have also the duty to create within the etheric atmosphere of the earth a balance for the tremendous forces of evil that have been let loose. Many years ago Rudolf Steiner already told his friends: 'Anthroposophy consists of the willingness to do in a spirit of devotion and sacrifice what our time demands of us!'

Those inspiring perspectives Rudolf Steiner has given of the new working of Christ within the realm of spiritual life should equally be taken as a challenge to the will to help in karmic solidarity: 'Now begins the significant time when Christ becomes Lord of Karma, when it will be up to Him in future to *determine* our karmic account: how our debit relates to our credit.'[21]

'Human beings of our time will learn that Christ will reveal Himself more and more supersensibly and will increasingly *have in His rule* the threads of karma in matters of the earth. Thus one learns to love karma; and this then becomes the impulse to recognize Christ!'[22]

III
The Michael Impulse

Deepened by the forces of the heart, cognition can lead to the conviction that the new Christ Impulse, able to transform destiny, can become fully effective among human beings on earth when they are ready to make a sacrifice for it. Everything on earth must be earned. By whom it is earned, that is in the end all the same. Something specific can be earned for one individual by another. Thus we begin to see that the experience and enacting of moral freedom is henceforth to enter quite a new, higher stage.

Christ also wants to become on earth more and more the Genius of freedom through grace. Human beings will attain a freer relationship to destiny in the measure in which they strive to feel responsible to Christ in thoughts, feelings, words and deeds. To this necessity, too, Rudolf Steiner pointed earlier. For in this, too, is expressed the fact that Christ within the supersensible earth has now become Lord and Guide of the forces of karma: 'That human beings will develop a feeling of being accountable to Christ in everything they do.'

In those who want to cultivate such an attitude of soul, conscience will gradually condense into a special power of 'moral clairvoyance'. In the end a stage will be reached when images of conscience will be given to somebody who is about to perform an action, images revealing, as it were warningly, the karmic consequences of the intended deed, or else showing which deeds of compensation would have to be done later according to karmic laws. Thus the stage is gradually reached at which for human consciousness what is karmically necessary enters the realm of cognition and free will. Along this path, the experienced and even in part freely understood truths of karma become *the foundation of all future morality and religion*.

As early on as 1917 Rudolf Steiner remarked: 'The time is surely no longer far off when in the immortal part of their being people will question what they intend to bring about—"Shall it be done? Shall it not be done?"—when the human soul will see Christ close by as a loving companion in each event of life, and will receive not only comfort, not only strength, but also instruction as to what should be done. The Kingdom of Christ Jesus is not *of* this world, but it has to work *in* this world, and human souls must become tools of this kingdom which is not of this world.' Mankind has to strive towards this goal. The new, fully human freedom will lie in our consciousness, facing life-situations: Not that which my limited personal ego wants shall be done, but that which Christ wants in me and through me.

*

This is what the apostles of Christ Jesus experienced under the influence of special grace, and this is what will be experienced again, though in a different form, in the new Christ Age which we have already entered. All the indications of Rudolf Steiner as to the present-day importance of St Paul's conversion at Damascus point in this direction!

Mankind has had to travel a long and very wearisome path of the soul until today when human beings have awakened to the consciousness of this responsibility towards Christ Who is spiritually present. They set out along this path when the power of thought awakened in them.

In the primeval past mankind had eaten from the tree of knowledge. The deceptive Light Spirit had seduced it to do this. That cosmic enthusiast for freedom had not been able to wait until God would lead human beings to true freedom (namely, out of love).

The first form of the power of freedom, the egoistic form,

thus came directly from Lucifer. Yet Rudolf Steiner pointed out: 'That spiritual power which has organized the Luciferic beings to enter into the formation of the head is the Michael power. "And he cast his opposing spirits down upon the earth." That means: Through this casting down of the Luciferic beings opposing Michael, man was first filled with reason, with what comes from the human head.'[23]

Apart from the primeval time, the permeation of the human head with Luciferic light has actually taken place twice, namely, in those periods in which the Archangel Michael was the regent of mankind. First, in the Michael Age of antiquity (around 600–250 BC) for the preparation of the Mystery of Golgotha, and now again today, to introduce the *new* Age of Christ. In the first period the birth of philosophy took place. Behind it, impulsating it, worked the two powers of light, not only Apollo-Michael but also Lucifer, as one can clearly see in the Greek enthusiasm for art.[24]

In the nineteenth century the second 'enlightenment' of the head led to the observation of thinking and cognition by means of many epistemological investigations. In his *Philosophy of Spiritual Activity* Rudolf Steiner continued these investigations in a Michaelic spirit, showing how the intellectual thinking of the head can be transformed into the clairvoyant thinking of the heart.

Now the time has come to enliven and spiritualize the intellect which is already hardening again. The time has come to transform the formal power of thought through love into its intuitive form and to intensify the power of will, active in thinking, into clairvoyant thinking (Imagination). 'Upon this fact, that the ideas of the human being do not remain only thoughts but become *a seeing within thinking,* immeasurably much depends.'

Those paths of the soul ultimately enable us in supersensible perception to behold the spiritual and to grasp the material as an expression of the spiritual: 'Michael must permeate us as the strong force which can grasp the material world, *in that it sees in the material at the same time the spiritual, in that within the material everywhere the spirit is seen.'*

In the future one should no longer first (pre-consciously) divide 'uniform reality' into a material and a spiritual part (sensory and conceptual worlds) in order then to relate them to each other anew. One will have to behold it as *uniform reality*, namely an *etheric essence*, sensory-super-sensible, imaginative. When you behold in the spiritual that which passes into the material and works within it, you are immersed in the true, creative existence of things. Precisely in this the Michael culture arises which stands in the Christian sign of the Scales, in that sign of equilibrium indicating to us the cosmic background of the higher unity of sensual and spiritual within the essence of the etheric.

*

The Michael Impulse, newly working since 1879, prepared for the new Christ Impulse which stands behind it the ways from Heaven into the earthly consciousness of the human being. First this had to be awakened!

In the sign of Michael Rudolf Steiner *founded* anthroposophy. In the sign of Christ he still has to *bring it to completion* in this century — in religious inwardness.

On the path of cognition outwards, through perception and thinking, Michael can become the helper of man as far as the stage of Imagination. A spiritually orientated knowledge of Nature and cosmology is the fruit of it.

On the path inwards, into the depths of the human soul where Christ lives, inspiration of the heart will stir in the human being when he turns in reverence to Christ. 'Through the right relationship to Christ, in the living intercourse of the soul with Him, the human being will experience what otherwise he could only receive as the traditional revelation of faith. The inner world of the life of soul will be experienced as illumined by the spirit even as the outer world of nature is seen as carried by the spirit.'[25]

Without an energetic and enthusiastic life of thinking and without an upright, active love for our fellow human beings we will not get further on either path. But if we can mingle both attitudes of soul with each other, then gradually the *resurrection* of thinking from death will take place, and thereby the return of intelligence to the fiery, radiating spirituality of Uriel, whose administrator is the Archangel Michael, according to Rudolf Steiner.

It is a way of self-transformation, enabling the soul to receive enlightenment from the cosmic Spirit Self. But today it is indeed a matter of the existence or non-existence of the true human self.

Mankind as a whole has already unconsciously crossed the threshold and is therefore suffering hardship. Perhaps each one of us will soon be led into the severe soul testing of consciously crossing the threshold.

Michael wants human beings courageously to overcome the weakening consequences of the Fall through thinking and action so that they can *unite* themselves with God. His goal for human beings is God-humanity. Hence his bold watchword: 'Who is like God?'

As the 'Angel of God' Michael was the protective genius of the old covenant between God and the people of Israel, God's people, who arose from the bloodline of the twelve sons of Jacob. Today, however, as the messenger of Christ, Michael strengthens the endeavours of all those human beings who want to become courageous 'fighters of God' for the *new* Christ Impulse and the revelation of the eternal Gospel. They will become the 'New Israel'.

*

Especially from 1923 onwards, for the pupils of Rudolf Steiner to form a fearless Michael knighthood has shone out as the highest goal. Only Michaelites can today unite in

Christ a humanity which is disastrously split up into national egoisms. This is the longing of countless people today. There are for sure many more Michaelites, courageous fighters for the spirit, also in the whole of Eastern Europe where it is forbidden to cultivate anthroposophy.* Let us not forget these suffering brothers and sisters!

Today, in the sense of the Apocalypse, it is our task to unite in the spiritual brotherhood of the 'New Israel'.[26]

---

* Publisher's note: This was, of course, written before the collapse of the Communist U.S.S.R. in 1989.

IV
The Grail Impulse

The purifying transformation of human nature through the ego starts in the soul and then reaches deeper and deeper into the unconscious members. Of the supersensible-sensory sheaths, the power of the physical body will be the last to be transformed into divine archetypal beinghood. Then will the 'last enemy' — death — be overcome.

First and archetypal among all resurrected ones is the Jesus Individuality who was awakened from death on Golgotha by the Father God. He is the eternal bearer of the Christ Spirit. Early Christian knowledge as well as the anthroposophical knowledge of man let us recognize: The 'other Adam', who summoned St Paul, was the archetype of man who had remained pure. Christ Jesus is the representative of mankind.

That original Adam, as Rudolf Steiner has shown, was a truly divine superhuman being. Even before His earthly incarnation, which was to rescue the ego of man, the Jesus Being had undertaken a threefold sacrifice for mankind in the supersensible realm. The human bodily sheaths were healed from the worst consequences of the Fall of man.

Rudolf Steiner revealed this holy secret in the 'Grail' cycle of lectures *Christ and the Spiritual World*.[27] There he showed us: That divine, archetypal being of man is itself the Holy Grail as a spiritual being. After the painful death of sacrifice and triumphant resurrection the hands of angels carried the Grail, the Resurrected One, from the hill of Golgotha over to Europe, where the Grail Temple was erected for Him within the etheric realm of the earth.

Since the eighth century those Christian souls have been able to find it who, in the spirit of St Paul, were able to purify their blood. The personal ego, although then not yet fully developed, let alone hardened, prepared itself in such human beings, offering to become a chalice for receiving the Christ Will. For them St Paul's words became true again: I live, though actually not I, but Christ in me.

Thus in the knights of the Grail was shown 'how the higher ego of man, how the divine spirit of mankind, which through the event of Palestine was born in Jesus of Nazareth, had remained the same and had been retained with those who had the right understanding for it. In the Grail it was retained, with the Grail it remained connected.'[28]

One of the many legendary images of the Grail says: It was formed into a chalice out of the precious stone which fell from Lucifer's crown when Michael fought with him in heaven. That jewel, so Rudolf Steiner once remarked, is 'in a certain respect nothing other than the full power of the human ego'. The image of the chalice of the Last Supper, in which Joseph of Arimathea gathered the blood of the Redeemer, points to the being of the Grail itself, the divine Jesus-ego, the bearer of the God-ego, of the life of the sun, of the blood of the sun.

However, it points at the same time to all those human souls who purify themselves in their heart's blood and behold God because they have prepared themselves through sacrifice to be a vessel for the impulses of Christ.

In 'blissful longing' Goethe's 'die and become', truly in the sense of St John, proclaimed the necessity for the self-sacrifice of the human soul. The soul is to become a phoenix. Only he who loses his life of self, only he who gives up his existence, will win the true life, will earn his higher existence in freedom.

The personally tinted experience of freedom, again and again tending to arbitrariness, is still a Luciferic heritage. Only those ideas and impulses, proceeding from Intuition permeated by love, are graced by the Christ-freedom.

Love is the being of the Grail which begins to grow in us. The innermost life of the soul, the being of the ego, is indeed love or the power of Intuition, as Rudolf Steiner and before him J. G. Fichte have proclaimed. Goethe's words describe this freedom: 'Everything arbitrary and imagined collapses; there is necessity, there is God.' This also points to new sources of all artistic creativity. The artist of the future works out of the motto of the Grail: Die and become. After all, according to our conviction, art is meant to lift the world up into the divine sphere or conjure up reality for our senses in such a way that it presents itself as an ideal world. The natural, the individual, should appear in an eternal garment fitted out with the character of the idea! Through the arts everything natural should already partake in a preliminary and forecasting way in the enlightened life of resurrection![29]

Both the enthusiast for freedom and the artist will want to remain ever mindful of the Grail Words that Rudolf Steiner spoke at the end of the 'resurrection' cycle (*From Jesus to Christ*):[30] In the centre of all our feelings the thought should live, 'You may reach human dignity; only one thing you must not forget: You owe what you are to Him Who has given you back your human archetype through the redemption on Golgotha. Human beings should not be able to think of freedom without thinking of the redemption of Christ. Only then is the thought of freedom justified. If we want to be free we have to make the sacrifice of owing our freedom to Christ. Then only can we truly perceive it.'

Freedom is a gift of grace from Christ. Rudolf Steiner noted in the fourth lecture that it would be necessary to exercise the concept of grace very practically. 'And every occultist today is clear about this: The concept of grace must belong in a very special degree to the conduct of his inner life.'

From the end of the nineteenth century up to the great world catastrophes—so terribly shameful and humiliating for humanity—it was utterly necessary to stress the ego's own creative power. Today, where this development has often gone too far in the direction of outrageous haughtiness and the Cain element has become all too strong, it is just as important to stress the impulse of moderation towards which Thomas à Kempis can encourage us if we want to live in the sense of *The Imitation of Christ*, as also in the sense of *Knowledge of the Higher Worlds*.

That the ego has become the true source of freedom through having filled itself with Christ is the very reason for freedom realizing itself in its purest form in sacrificial acts. 'Like an empty vessel (no Grail chalice) the ego would have become without Christ; like a vessel filling itself more and more with love, the ego stands there through the appearance of Christ.'[31] Are we sufficiently conscious of this truth about the ego? Or does perhaps a certain exaggeration in our thinking sometimes tempt us to feel we owe freedom to ourselves?

*

We of the present time must work again today at the invisible temple of the Grail. One millennium after Parzival and Lohengrin, many are called to be new seekers of the Grail. May these words show us the direction: 'All that happens here through love, through friendship, through deep mutual understanding, these are the building stones for temples up there in the spiritual region!'

May the human community of 'Philadelphia', in whose representatives is inscribed the name of the *New Jerusalem* (Revelation III, 12), daily become ever more decisively our high goal.

May we thus be shown the way from the free consciousness soul to the spirit-self united with the world, which becomes capable of the highest freedom. 'The greatest freedom, my dear friends, is given when one does what is necessary for world history!' (See the whole context of this in the fourth lecture of *Necessity and Freedom*.)[32]

Only in continuously overcoming one's self does the transformation of astral body into spirit-self take place!

But it is even more difficult to spiritualize the etheric and physical bodies and change them back into those cosmic spiritual members from which they have arisen. Ultimately this leads to the resurrection of the flesh and the overcoming of death.

Along this path the ego meets something which is initially not under its control. This was pointed to with great earnestness in the lectures on *Mysteries of the East and of Christianity*.[33]

'Whereas the human being can, on the one hand, become ever more free, Ahrimanic and Luciferic powers creep into what has been removed from the rulership of the soul.' Because the *old star wisdom* of the age of Isis — which formerly kept the etheric-physical body alive and healthy — has long been forgotten, those counter-forces have been able to attach themselves so fatally to that part of human nature which has become unconscious, and there build the castle of Christ's opponents: Chastel Merveil, the Castle of Wonders.

On the other hand, from Montsalvasch, Salvation Mount, where the guardians and caretakers of the Grail hold sway, proceeds the *new wisdom of the stars*, the centre of which is the Sun Spirit, Christ. In this school one can learn 'what one has to pour into that part of the soul which has remained alive, in order to become master over what has become dead in the physical body and unconscious in the soul. Therefore even in the Middle Ages the seer pointed to the castle of the Holy Grail and to the *new wisdom* — which is indeed the Grail! — that emanated from this castle.'

Even though the high ideal of Philadelphia (brotherly love) can only be fully realized by the progressive part of mankind in the sixth (Slavic) cultural epoch, nevertheless already in the present fifth cultural period (Sardis) mankind has received from the sphere of the *Sophia* that knowledge which enables us to fulfil the command of the Angel: 'Cultivate wakeful consciousness and strengthen what is still alive in your soul, in order that it does not also die.'

V

The Sophia Impulse

Characterizing the symbol of the Grail, Rudolf Steiner said: 'That precious stone is in a certain respect nothing other than the full power of the human ego'.[34]

'This human ego first had to be prepared in darkness in order to see the star of Lucifer shine in a new, worthy way. This ego had to educate itself upwards through the Christ principle, had to mature through the precious stone which has fallen from the crown of Lucifer; it had to mature through wisdom, through theosophy.'

We see in the epistles of St Paul the first seeds of the Christ Theosophy, inspired by the Sophia. One should read the first epistle to the Corinthians as well as the epistles to the Ephesians and Colossians. A further development of that wisdom is to be found in the ninth century in the writings of Scotus Erigena concerning the Resurrection, in his views of the divinity of man and cosmos. Today we have the wisdom of spiritual science.

The Grail cycle of lectures[35] speaks mainly about the pre-earthly deeds of sacrifice of the Jesus Individuality. This is the Individuality Who is meant by the precious stone that has come to earth out of the zodiacal crown of heaven. This archetypal being of the ego-soul came from the direction of the Fishes; that is why the Fisher King and also the Fish as such play important roles in the legends of the Grail.[36]

To the Fishes in the zodiac belongs the opposite constellation of the Virgin: a cosmic polarity of utmost importance which also plays a prominent role in the Feeding Imagination of the Gospels. In primeval times the Virgin was the constellation of Lucifer. However, the divine

Sophia is more and more coming to take his place. She is the inspirer of the science of the Grail.

Therefore — with reference to the gnosis of Valentinus, to which also the *Pistis-Sophia* is related — the first lecture of the Grail cycle shows how out of divine, pre-worldly emanations of aeons (from the hidden primeval being up to supersensible mankind) has sprung the higher, the sublime Sophia, as it were the sister-being of the Star of Jesus, in which we recognize the Grail Chalice of the Son of God.

At the end of those lectures, following on from the image of Sigune with the slain Schionatulander on her lap, Rudolf Steiner lets us surmise the uncommonly sublime importance of the Pieta Imagination: In esotericism the pure virgin mother Mary is called 'the virgin Sophia'! Therefore the following profound words are related to her, but also to her heavenly primeval image, the divine Sophia: 'Let us place before ourselves the mother, thought of as a virgin, with Christ on her lap, and let us then make the statement: He who can have feelings of holiness before this image, he feels himself to be standing before the Grail. The holy chalice, the moon-mother now touched by Christ, the new Eve, bearer of Christ the Sun Spirit, outshines all other lights, all other gods.'

Jesus Himself, the Resurrected One, the Phoenix Being, is the holy Grail, but the Sophia is the inspirer of the wisdom of the Grail.

The Archangel Michael is also most deeply linked with the Sophia. Rudolf Steiner derived the Greek name of primeval wisdom as follows: For the Babylonian people of olden times, Ea was the name of the god of wisdom and friend of man. By prefixing this name with the particle 'soph' (meaning 'being', 'existing'), the word 'Soph-ea' or 'Soph-ia' (a foreign word for the Greeks) came about: the ruling wisdom as the Godhead. The Babylonian wise men saw the God Marduk, whom we today call Michael, as a scion of Ea. His son, however, was Nabu or Nebo, god of clairvoyance, of prophecy.

Christ-Michael and the Sophia are working, inspiring, in spirit-union. Through this the wisdom of the Grail comes about.

*

Rudolf Steiner pointed to that Being of Wisdom much more often than one thinks. Of course he meant her whenever he spoke of the creative 'primeval wisdom'. Within herself, this Being carries and cares for the plan of world development in its essence. This is spun out in the sphere 'above the region of Intuition'. In this plan, the spiritual tasks of all human beings are united in an overall image. This points to divine Providence! Thus, in the sense of the Sophia, also the powers of karma work together with the Christ Spirit Who is *reversing* directions of karma!

*

With special emphasis Rudolf Steiner pointed to the Sophia when he wanted to lead his listeners to the original sources of anthroposophy. This happened most strikingly when, after separating from the Theosophical Society, the Anthroposophical Society held its first general meeting on 3 February 1913. In the lecture he gave on the being of anthroposophy[37] Steiner showed how the Sophia was a living, deeply revered being, a sublime goddess to people of the Middle Ages as also to the Greeks of olden times. At the end he spoke of what this Sophia ought to mean for us now:

'But human beings have learnt to relate this Sophia to their own consciousness soul, to bring her near to them in an immediate way. This has happened during the age of the consciousness soul. Thereby the Sophia has become the immediate being who *explains* what the human being is. After she has entered into man she must take along his being and place it objectively before him once again. She will free herself but take along the human being and present herself objectively, now not only as the Sophia but as

Anthropos-Sophia, as that Sophia who, after having gone through the soul of man, through the being of man, forthwith carries this being within herself.'

Soon afterwards Rudolf Steiner went a step further. In a lecture on 10 January 1915 he described what kind of being this Sophia is within the divine world.[38] She reveals herself out of the hierarchy of the primeval sunlike Spirits of Wisdom. Living in the Christ-hierarchy of the 'Kyrios' and Kyriotetes she becomes as it were the sister-being of the Sun Spirit, Christ. In that lecture we find among other things:

The Sophia Being has a biography in which she reveals herself through all the members of the human being, one after the other, each in a different way. For the development of the human soul a seven-year period is the time in which one human member unfolds. For the infinitely sublime Christ-related divine being such an unfolding takes 700 years. From the time of Abraham (about 2100 BC) the Sophia Being began to reveal herself to mankind, bestowing wisdom. Today she has thus reached her 'fortieth year of life'. Ultimately the four phases of philosophical thought must be grasped on the basis of this development.[39]

Out of the primeval world-wisdom of the Orient, in the course of septennates of aeons, there gradually arose within human consciousness the merely thought-oriented seeking for wisdom, the love for the Sophia (Philosophy). At the beginning of modern times (around 1400) this Sophia began to mirror herself in the consciousness soul. This member of our being bound to the physical body is indeed a very narrow and dark gate! Since then the once living and inspiring wisdom has had to fade away within the heads of human beings. In the nineteenth century it was threatened with extinction.[40]

But at that very moment, as a fruit of Christ's sacrifice in love, there awoke in man the youthful power of freedom and spiritual creativity of the ego.

The Christian initiate of the present time has awakened

dying thinking to new spirit life. This has led to the rebirth of the Sophia out of the depths of the human being! She has become Anthropos-Sophia! At the moment when even the shadowy remnants of the Sophia's manifestation threatened to die away at the end of the nineteenth century, Rudolf Steiner enacted the resurrection of the Sophia-consciousness within the ego out of the Michael-Christ Impulse. Here is how he wanted the word 'anthroposophy' to be understood:

'Anthroposophy should be nothing other than the Sophia, namely that content of consciousness inwardly experienced in the constitution of the human soul which makes the human being fully human. The right interpretation of the word "anthroposophy" is not "wisdom of man" but "*consciousness of man's being human*".'

The turning of the will inwards, the experience of cognition and the involvement with the destiny of the time, are meant to aim at giving the soul a direction of consciousness, a Sophia.

It is not the reality of Christ that is missing in the present civilization, as Rudolf Steiner said on another occasion, but the wisdom of the knowledge of Christ and linked with this the consciousness of the true being of man. Everyone who has found anthroposophy owes to it the new knowledge of the being of man and of Christ.

In this connection we point to the lectures on *The Search for the New Isis, the Divine Sophia* (1920),[41] and also to *Ancient Myths. Their Meaning and Connection with Evolution* (1917).[42] But we can only quote very essential groups of sentences. 'I wish to say: We seek Pallas Athene, we seek the virgin wisdom, the virgin wisdom of the cosmos – but also the Son descended from her. He expresses himself thus: In everything we want to do in social life this wisdom plays a part and forms the direction for our activity. Then we express the Spirit, to be precise the Holy Spirit, in sensory actions on the physical plane.'

To this belong those other, exceptionally important words: *'These three: inspiring spirit, virgin mother and the Logos or Word, they are indeed to be held on to; they must also be sought through anthroposophical spiritual science.'*

*

The Sophia Being was already known to some wise men of the Old Testament. With greatest reverence they looked up to her, praising her in hymns as the archetypal artist working and creating together with Jehovah, as a friend of man and inspirer of prophets and seers. Highest goodness and wisdom are united within her incomprehensibly lofty being.

Unfortunately writings by such wise men as Solomon (Proverbs, Chapter 7; Wisdom, Chapter 8), Job (Chapter 28), and Jesus of Sirach (Ecclesiasticus, Chapter 24), have been nearly forgotten or else inadequately translated. All these bear witness to her. Lovers of wisdom can find those testimonials fittingly honoured in M. Friedländer's *Griechische Philosophie im Alten Testament* (1904).

The hymns of Solomon also let us divine something of that supra-hierarchical archetypal Being, that Queen of the Stars, to whom also Rudolf Steiner wished to point in speaking of the 'archetypal wisdom'. Among other things he said: 'Before our world existed, there existed that wisdom of which we actually have to speak. *It is the plan of the world.'*[43]

*

The light of the new wisdom lets us recognize the true being of Christ and of man, the Anthropos. Its fruit can and shall always be *love*: the power of the divine Son of the Sophia.

Two main thoughts can warm the soul as the heart's blood of anthroposophy: 'We know and must confess that we could not be as the human soul should be, if this human soul could not be filled with love. Indeed, in entering the being of the soul we discover that it could not remain a human soul if it were unable to love.'

That is the one thought, to which we add the other: 'After all, our teaching itself is that which Christ has wanted to say to us, fulfilling his words: "I am with you always even unto the end of the earth." We have only wanted to listen to what comes from Him. What He has inspired in us, according to His promise, we want to take into our souls as our spiritual science.'[44]

*

One can today only find the way to Christ in spirit in so far as one is able to confront and wrestle with the counter-forces of the soul: with Lucifer and Ahriman. In wrestling for equilibrium one is helped from above most strongly against the predominance of the Luciferic temptation to haughtiness and fanaticism by the Grail Impulse and the still much higher Sophia Impulse. Against the predominance of the Ahrimanic spell, however, one is helped by the Michael Impulse and the still much higher Impulse of the Powers of Karma. Together with the Christ Impulse at the centre they form the present impulse of Christ for the free human ego.

*

The holy Sophia, together with the Christ Spirit, has always been highly revered among Christian Slavs. During the epoch of 'brotherly love' (Philadelphia) those Slavs are destined to become the main bearers of the revelation of the spirit-self within the soul. Only through the fulfilment of the spirit-self will it become possible to experience anew the Sophia also in her original heavenly glory. This will already begin in the coming septennate of aeons of her revelation through the members of the human being. The septennate of the spirit-self begins in the year 2100, when the first third of the fifth cultural epoch will be over. Its first half will end around the year 2500.

In his lectures on *The Mission of the Individual Folk Souls*[45] Rudolf Steiner also had important things to say about the folk spirit of Central Europe, which from now onwards should be very much taken to heart: 'He is especially able to bring about what could not as yet be given in the first half [of the fifth cultural epoch] but can still come about in the second, namely what can be shown as a spiritual element, as a prophetic seed, in the Slavic philosophy and the sensibility of the Slavic people.'

*

May the souls in Central Europe who have been touched by Anthropos-Sophia not forget the Eastern Europeans, whose prayers have been rising up to the holy Sophia in inward fervour perhaps already for many years.

Those who venerate the Spirit in West and East should now, when the new Christ-Age has dawned, soon find each other in understanding in the sign of Michael and Uriel.

Much can be contributed to this if, for the sake of mankind, many students of anthroposophy will turn to the impulses or inspirations working within it: those of the Beings of Karma, of the Sophia, of Christ, of Michael, and of the Grail.

This brings them into harmony with their spiritual leader.

Notes and Bibliography

1 R. Steiner *The Fifth Gospel* (GA 148). London: Rudolf Steiner Press 1995.

2 S. von Gleich *De Heilige Graal en de Nieuwe Tijd van Christus* (privately published Zeist 1952).

3 R. Steiner *Occult Science and Occult Development* (in GA 152). London: Rudolf Steiner Press 1983, lecture of 2 May 1913.

4 R. Steiner *Toward Imagination* (GA 169). Hudson: Anthroposophic Press 1990.

5 R. Steiner *Awakening to Community* (GA 257). New York: Anthroposophic Press 1974, lecture of 30 January 1923.

6 R. Steiner *The Younger Generation* (GA 217). New York: Anthroposophic Press 1984.

7 R. Steiner *Metamorphoses of the Soul. Paths of Experience*, Vol.1. (GA 59). London: Rudolf Steiner Press 1983, lecture of 28 October 1909 entitled 'The Mission of Reverence'.

8 R. Steiner *From Jesus to Christ* (GA 131). London: Rudolf Steiner Press 1991, lecture of 8 October 1911.

9 R. Steiner *The Inner Nature of Man and our Life Between Death and a New Birth* (GA 153). Bristol: Rudolf Steiner Press 1994, lecture of 12 April 1914.

10 R. Steiner *Anthroposophical Leading Thoughts* (GA 26). London: Rudolf Steiner Press 1973.

11 R. Steiner *From Jesus to Christ*, op. cit., lecture of 7 October 1911.

12 W. Soloviev *Ausgewählte Werke*, Jena 1914. Essay entitled 'Das Bild Christi als eine Prüfung des Gewissens' (The image of Christ as a test of conscience).

13 R. Steiner *From Jesus to Christ*, op. cit., lecture of 7 October 1911.

14 R. Steiner *Occult Science and Occult Development*, op. cit., lecture of 2 May 1913.

15 In *Das Goetheanum*, No. 30 & 31, 1951.

16 R. Steiner *Reincarnation and Karma* (GA 135). N. Vancouver: Steiner Book Centre 1977.

17 R. Steiner *Karmic Relationships, Vol. 1.* (GA 235). London: Rudolf Steiner Press 1972, lecture of 2 March 1924.

18 S. von Gleich 'Die überpersönliche Lebensbestimmung' in *Mitteilungen aus der anthroposophischen Arbeit in Deutschland,* No. 22, 1952. S. von Gleich *Die Umwandlung des Bösen,* Basle: Zbinden Verlag 1975.

19 R. Steiner *At the Gates of Spiritual Science* (GA 95). London: Rudolf Steiner Press 1986, lecture of 27 August 1906.

20 R. Steiner *The Gospel of St Matthew* (GA 123). New York: Anthroposophic Press 1985, lecture of 11 September 1910.

21 R. Steiner *From Jesus to Christ,* op. cit, lecture of 7 October 1911.

22 R. Steiner *The Three Paths of the Soul to Christ* (in GA143). New York, Anthroposophic Press 1942, lecture of 17 April 1912.

23 R. Steiner *Ideas for a New Europe* (in GA 194). Forest Row: Rudolf Steiner Press 1992, lectures of 12–15 December 1919.

24 S. von Gleich *Mysterien-Dämmerung und Christus-Erscheinung.* Stuttgart: J. Ch. Mellinger Verlag 1973.

25 R. Steiner *Anthroposophical Leading Thoughts,* op. cit.

26 *Book of Revelation,* Chap. VII; see also E. Bock *The Apocalypse of St John,* London: Christian Community Press 1957.

27 R. Steiner *Christ and the Spiritual World and The Search for the Holy Grail* (GA 149). London: Rudolf Steiner Press 1983.

28 R. Steiner *The Gospel of St John and its Relation to the Other Gospels* (GA 112). New York: Anthroposophic Press 1982.

29 R. Steiner *Goethe as Founder of a New Science of Aesthetics.* (in GA 30). London: Anthroposophical Publishing Co. 1922.

30 R. Steiner *From Jesus to Christ* (GA 131), op. cit., lecture of 14 October 1911.

31 R. Steiner *The Gospel of St Luke* (GA 114). London: Rudolf Steiner Press and New York: Anthroposophic Press 1988, lecture of 25 September 1909.

32 R. Steiner *Necessity and Freedom* (GA 166). New York: Anthroposophic Press 1988, lecture of 1 February 1916.

33 R. Steiner *Mysteries of the East and of Christianity* (GA 144) Blauvelt: Garber Communications Inc. 1989.

34 R. Steiner *The East in the Light of the West* (GA 113). Blauvelt: Garber Communications Inc. 1986, lecture of 23 August 1909.

35   R. Steiner *Christ and the Spiritual World and The Search for the Holy Grail*, op. cit.

36   R. Steiner *Background to the Gospel of St Mark* (GA 124). New York: Anthroposophic Press and London: Rudolf Steiner Press 1985.

37   The lecture of 3 February 1913 is entitled 'Schicksalszeichen auf dem Entwicklungswege der Anthroposophischen Gesellschaft'. It is available in English as Typescript S11 at Rudolf Steiner House Library, London.

38   R. Steiner *Wege der geistigen Erkenntnis und der Erneuerung künstlerischer Weltanschauung* (GA 161). Dornach: Rudolf Steiner Verlag 1980, lecture of 10 January 1915.

39   R. Steiner *Riddles of Philosophy* (GA 18). New York: Anthroposophic Press 1973.

40   About the periods of development see: S. von Gleich 'Die Menschenseele, der Stern und die himmlische Weisheit' in *Blätter für Anthroposophie*, No. 1, 1951, and 'Die drei Gottesbünde und die Sophia' in ibid. No. 5, 1951.

41   R. Steiner *The Search for the New Isis, the Divine Sophia* (in GA 202). Spring Valley: Mercury Press 1983.

42   R. Steiner *Ancient Myths. Their Meaning and Connection with Evolution* (GA 180). New York: Anthroposophic Press 1994.

43   R. Steiner *The Spiritual Hierarchies and the Physical World* (GA 110). Hudson: Anthroposophic Press 1996, lecture of 12 April 1909.

44   R. Steiner *Christ and the Human Soul* (in GA 155). London: Rudolf Steiner Press 1984.

45   R. Steiner *The Mission of the Individual Folk Souls* (GA 121). London: Rudolf Steiner Press 1970.